Betsy Patterson has placed her life in God's hands. She has never been disappointed in her loving faith:

I call them minies, the tiny miracles that come from
    God's hand.
If you do not know Jesus personally you will not
    understand—
It's the little things I see him in, that are very precious
    to me.
Many do not notice them because they are not looking,
    you see.
Put God into *every* detail—put him first in everything.
Then you'll see minies in your life which cause your
    heart to sing.

JESUS

—My Life And My Love

BETSY PATTERSON

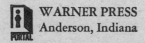

WARNER PRESS
Anderson, Indiana

JESUS—MY LIFE AND MY LOVE

A PORTAL BOOK
Published for Warner Press, Inc., by Pyramid Publications

Portal Books edition published January, 1975

ISBN 0-87162-179-7

Printed in the United States of America

PORTAL BOOKS are published by Warner Press, Inc.
1200 East 5th Street, Anderson, Indiana 46011, U.S.A.

To the Honor and Glory of God the Father
God the Son
God the Holy Spirit

Dedicated to my beloved husband, Jack,
who has relinquished first place in my
life to "Jesus—My Life and My Love"

To My Husband, Jack

As for God his way is perfect!
he brought *us* together in love divine.
How can we doubt it—the Master mind.
In all, over all, and around all,
Always there whenever we call,
Such depth of love *we* know
All because our God is Love, and so—
So great a love that he gave his only son for you
and me
That we might be together on earth and through-
out all eternity.
What he suffered on the cross for our sins makes us
sad—
But his resurrection is the good news that makes us
glad—
Oh, what riches now are *ours* if we but let him have
his way
In our lives; surrendering our wills, our intellects,
our very selves—then he'll say
"My death was not in vain.
Seeing you two in one, in me, takes away all pain."

Acknowledgments

Carol Seaman, Betty Ross, and Mil Gerig gave of their precious time to help in the preparation of this manuscript. They each stated they did it to the glory of God! My personal thanks to each of them is expressed beautifully in the words of Paul: "Grace be unto you, and peace, from God our Father, and from the Lord Jesus Christ. I thank my God upon every remembrance of you, always in every prayer of mine for you all making request with joy" (Phil. 1:2-4).

I thank Jack, my loving husband, for permitting me to go to the beautiful island of Hilton Head, South Carolina, to write. Another thank you for the constant and invaluable encouragement he gave me.

And to Angie, our daughter, a big thanks to you for taking care of dad and our home.

My deep appreciation is extended to all my dear friends behind the scenes who gave of themselves in prayer for the writing of the book and for me.

Jesus—My Life and My Love

Preface

"You mean you have the audacity to entertain the thought of writing another book? The first one, *The Valley of Vision*, isn't in the hands of a publisher as yet." These words awakened me in the wee hours of the morning. I immediately recognized them to be from the evil one. He was attempting to change my thoughts. He was twisting the ideas the Lord was giving to me at that moment. I rebuked the devil just as Jesus did on the mount of temptation (Matt. 4:10). I said, "Lord, *I am* going to write the second book. You have told me to." Just the day before in my quiet moments with him he had given me several special verses. I believed they were spoken directly to me as guidance. The verses were, "Take thee again another roll, and write in it" (Jer. 36:28). A second one was, "Be admonished: of making many books there is no end" (Eccles. 12:12).

Lying there in the darkness, my thoughts wandered back to the day the Lord gave me the title to the second book.

It happened like this. My husband and I were returning home from Wisconsin where I had completed the greater part of the rough draft of the first book. We were nearing Fort Wayne. Suddenly the words "my life and my love" were repeated over and over again in my mind. It was like a broken record. I said "Lord, is this of you?" The still small voice of the Holy Spirit spoke. "Yes, this is to be the title of your second book." I was astounded that he would give me this future information. He usually requires me to take one step at a time.

My thoughts began to race. "Lord, are you really giving me the title to a second book when the first one isn't completed?" A deep sense of peace and assurance came over me. I knew it had been the Lord speaking. The second book would be written. However, every time I said, "My life and my love" I had a strange feeling the Lord was going to add something to it. Little did I know at that time how it was to come about.

The first book was published in September, 1973, by Warner Press, Anderson, Indiana. I began working on the second book before sending the first one to the publisher.

In November, 1973, I received a letter from Dr. Phillips, the editor-in-chief of Warner Press, stating he would like to take a peek into my second book. He was interested in some of my ideas for it.

On Wednesday afternoon my husband and I paid a visit to Dr. Phillips. The first question he asked was, "What is the title?" I told him and he said, "Do you plan to have each chapter relate to the title? We may want to change it." I said, "Oh, you can't change it because the Lord gave me the title."

He pondered a moment and said, "Betsy, what would you think of adding the word Jesus to the title? *Jesus—My Life and My Love*."

"Oh," I said, "*that's it!* I didn't think it was complete as it was, but I didn't know what was missing. Oh, thank you, Dr. Phillips. That's it: *Je-*

sus—*My Life and My Love*." I told him the Lord had already impressed me with the idea that each chapter title was to be just one word. Then I read aloud to him the one chapter I had completed— "Party!" When I finished he said, "Betsy, I think *you have* a second book." Thus the second book was born!

Looking to myself for words for the second book, I am helpless and weak. I know all his promises are "yea" and "amen." For the second book I am trusting in him and his promise. "For he performeth the thing that is appointed for me" (Job 23:14).

Contents

Chapter I

JESUS

"And she shall bring forth a son, and thou shalt call his name Jesus . . .

"Behold, a virgin shall be with child, and shall bring forth a son, and they shall call his name Emmanuel, which being interpreted is, God with us."

—Matthew 1:21, 23

Jesus is the most exciting person I've ever met! To know him personally is to love him. Each day is an adventure when I walk with my hand in his! I've been trusting him, listening to him, and obeying him for about twenty-one years. He has never failed me once when I truly trusted him. He says he will never leave us or forsake us (Heb. 13:5). I am writing this chapter on Sunday, his day, as I look out over the Atlantic ocean. It is a beautiful day. How fantastic our Lord is if we will just permit him to have his way in our lives. I can't believe I am here. "But with God all things are possible" (Matt. 19:26). I tried writing this book at home. I simply couldn't concentrate. Just as a thought came, there was an interruption. My husband suggested I "get out of town" in a motel room where I would be completely alone.

13

Sue Hillery, a dear friend, had made a comment once that Hilton Head Island, South Carolina, was the closest place to heaven she had ever been. My husband and I came to the agreement that I should go there. Well, here I am! Jesus never makes a mistake. I know it's just where he wants me. I want to relate two tiny incidents that have happened in the short time I've been here. Through these Jesus has pointed out to me *once again* what real trusting is. At times I *think* I'm trusting him in every detail of my life and then I'm brought up short.

When I arrived at the Holiday Inn, I was impressed with the quietness and the seclusion. That night I began writing. Out of the blue, I heard a whining noise. It became louder and louder. Suddenly a bark. It was a dog and in the room next to mine. I was disturbed. However, the flow of words continued to come from the Lord. The dog finally gave up. His owners must have returned to the room. The next morning it started all over again. I said, "Lord, you brought me all the way down here from Fort Wayne to South Carolina to write your book and I'm going to have to put up with *that?*" The Holy Spirit's still small voice whispered, "Trust me, I'll take care of it." Still the dog continued to whine and bark.

When I went to breakfast I was tempted to stop at the desk and complain. I didn't. As I left the dining room after breakfast, I found the temptation too great. I yielded. I went to the girl at the desk and tried in a most amiable way to complain about the dog. She said, "We do allow dogs in the motel, but if they disturb any of our guests we notify the owners. We'll take care of it, ma'am."

I returned to my room and all was quiet. I thought, "My, that was fast work." The still small voice spoke to me again. "I took care of it. Why did you have to complain?" A few hours later I was called to the desk to pick up a letter. The same girl to whom I had complained said, "Ma'am, the couple who had the dog in the room next to you checked out right after you complained to me about their dog." I asked Jesus to forgive me for not trusting him in this. If I had only waited upon the Lord.

I hadn't been here long until I realized I had not brought a watch or an alarm clock with me. The first day I got by. How? I called the operator at the front desk whenever I wanted to know the time. I finally went to Jesus with this. "Jesus," I said, "you know I can't be pestering those people at the desk for the time. I don't know how you can keep me informed but I'm truly going to trust you to do it. As I got up from my knees, I happened to glance over at the television set. I seldom watch TV. I hadn't even bothered to look at it, for I was entranced with the beautiful waves washing up on shore. At the bottom of the TV panel, I noticed a little knob. I looked again and saw it was an AM-FM radio. I pulled out the knob and a voice said, "The time is now 2:50." Cold chills went all over me. I said, "Thank you, Jesus, you are so precious. I want to trust you more in all things."

A prayer of thanksgiving that Jesus answered last night is worthy of note. In this room are two large overstuffed chairs with a round table between them. A lovely chandelier hangs over the table. All this is in front of the large glass patio doors. The room has two beds. The Lord knew I would need that extra bed for my notes, papers, and books. The motel dining room was very cold. In my room a square hole was cut in the wall in which I could see wires. I came to the conclusion (a stupid one) that there was no heat in the building since it was not quite completed. It was fine during the day, but became very cold at night. I put on a heavy sweater and covered my legs with my coat while writing. First Thessalonians 5:18 says, "In everything give thanks." I was constantly murmuring, "Thank you, Lord, for the cold." Jesus then honored my prayer of thanksgiving. This is how he did it.

Before I left home Jack, my husband, and Angie, our sixteen-year-old daughter, and I celebrated his birthday. He's a Valentine. He took us out to dinner. All day I wondered what I would give him for his birthday. I became desperate because I knew I didn't have time to go shopping for a gift. I said, "Jesus, *what* will I give Jack?" The still small voice said, "A telephone call to him every night you are gone."

I thanked Jesus for this great idea. I put it all on a little note, put the note in a box, wrapped it, and gave it to him. He seemed very pleased.

When I was talking to my husband last night, I said, "Everything is great but I get so cold in the evenings." He replied, "Betts, they wouldn't open that motel without heat. Look around; there *has* to be a thermostat some place in that room." I promised him I would. As soon as I hung up, I jumped out of bed and began looking. How had I missed it! There it was, a large box-type heater and air-conditioner. Where was it? Behind one of those big chairs. I just couldn't believe I hadn't seen it. I thanked Jesus for honoring my prayer of thanksgiving. I also thanked him again for the idea of the telephone calls. He used one of the calls to answer my prayer.

Here at the motel I have been very conscious of

all the people around me. They seem so oblivious to God and his handiwork. This morning during breakfast in the dining room many were laughing and talking about their golf game. They talked about what they hoped their score would be today. They appeared not even to think about the fact that today was the Lord's day. Sunday, the Sabbath. I didn't notice anyone giving thanks for his food. I felt saddened that so many people are apparently going their own way. No thought of God—just self, business, and pleasure. I also had thoughts about this on the plane trip here. I was deep in this thought at one particular time when Jesus impressed me with the thought, "Betsy, you were there once, you were walking in their shoes. You were doing all the good things and the things you thought were right. Who were you doing them for? You were seeking after pleasure, a nice home, and so on. Didn't you think of me only when you were in a jam? Didn't you use me as a fire escape? Stop, Betsy, remember back when you were there." A verse popped into my mind, "Ye have not chosen me, but I have chosen you" (John 15:16). I asked Jesus, "Why did you choose me? I can't comprehend why you would choose me." He said, "Because you wanted to be chosen."

While I was sitting in that plane seat, Jesus closed out everything going on about me and gave me a very simple illustration regarding this scripture verse. To me it was beautiful and I knew it was to go into this book. He said, "As a child, with a group of children, you would decide to play a game. The game required the group to be divided into two sides. Two of you were selected by the children to choose up sides. You stood in a line facing each other. The two leaders took turns choosing kids for their sides. The leaders would say, 'Who wants to be on my side?' If you did, you raised your hand. Then you would walk across to where he was standing. Betsy, that's what I am saying to each person in the world. Who wants to be on my side? If a person says, 'I do' then I choose him."

I said, "Oh, Jesus, I see it! So simple but so great! It illustrates the plan of salvation in such a simple way. Jesus, you give everyone a free choice! We can choose you and come over to your side, follow you, and be your disciple or we can choose the prince of the world and be his follower. When you chose Peter and the other disciples, you said in essence, 'Do you want to come over on my side?' They dropped everything and said, 'Yes, Jesus, we want to follow you.' "

I have four brothers, two of whom are with Jesus. They are Chester, Wallace, Paul, and Harry. Wallace chose Jesus and his way when he was young. I never knew the details of his conversion. He died when he was twenty-three. Chester, my oldest brother, went to join Jesus in September, 1973, just a few months ago. Chester said he walked the sawdust trail, the term used in earlier days. More evangelists used tents in which to conduct their services then. They would pour sawdust over the ground before setting up the chairs. Chester walked down through the sawdust to the platform to accept Jesus as his Lord and Savior.

I had prayed and trusted the Lord for Paul's conversion. My heart jumped for joy when our family received the following letter from him in 1954. I will share excerpts from it. My prayer is that his letter may touch your heart. You may find yourself in similar circumstances.

"Dear sis, brother, and family,

I want you to know the Lord has changed my life completely! I never used to think about tithing to the church. I used to go to church perhaps once or twice a month. I always had an excuse not to go. I would either sleep or drink beer while Mary and the kids went. When I went, I would put two or three dollars into the collection plate, thinking I had squared myself with the Lord. I also would think of the things I could have done with the money had I not given it. I was on the night shift at work. There were many ministers on the night shift. They were always asking me questions and constantly bringing up tithing. It began to get to me. I kept telling myself we couldn't afford to tithe and yet I had not tried it.

"One night I took Lin, [his son,] to a cub scout rally. I had been drinking. When we came home, Lin told his mother that I embarrassed him and that he was ashamed of me. When Mary [his wife] told me that, it was like sticking a knife in my back. It was then I turned to God and accepted Christ as my personal Savior. I prayed, oh, how I prayed for help and guidance. It has been so easy with the Lord's help. I know one can stop drinking if he makes up his mind to and asks God's help. We are also giving ten percent of my salary to the Lord's work. I have received so many blessings since I received Jesus as my Savior. The peace of mind he gives me is worth everything!

God bless you all.
Paul."

Harry, my younger brother, had a different type of experience with Jesus. Every time I visited him and his family he would always want to talk about

Christianity. *He* would bring up the subject, but he always accused me of bringing it up. Leaving their home one evening after our usual argumentative discussion, I said, "Harry, I'm never going to talk to you again about the Lord. If and when you decide to accept Jesus, you can write and tell me about it."

In the meantime, mother had come to live with us. We were both praying for Harry. We prayed that he would accept Jesus and *know* he was a Christian. A short time later we received the following letter from him:

"Dear Mother and Betsy,

I have been going to church with Berdean [his wife] every Sunday evening. It seemed like each Sunday the minister was looking directly at me. I became very convicted. Last Sunday night I *knew* I had to go up to the altar. The minute I reached the altar I knew Jesus had come into my heart and life. I knew I was saved! Berdean went up with me. The entire church stayed and prayed. I dismissed the congregation with prayer. Can you imagine? I used to shrink to think of it. How the Lord can work if one will just let him. I testified that I had a Christian sister and mother who had been praying for my salvation. The minister made me promise I would write to you tonight. I kept my promise.

                                        Love,
                                        Harry."

Mother and I truly rejoiced! Now all her children had accepted Jesus, and our family would be together in heaven throughout eternity.

Do you know this exciting person Jesus as your Lord and Savior? If not, and you would like to, say,

"I choose you, Jesus, I want to be on your side."
Then pray this simple little prayer: Dear heavenly
Father, please forgive all my past sins. Please,
Jesus, come into my heart and into my life and
take over completely. I believe you have done what
I have asked. Thank you. I pray this in your name,
Jesus. Amen.

The next step is to share the decision you have
just made with someone else. Get a Bible and begin
to read it. Begin in the New Testament. John is a
good book with which to begin. Pray. Talk to your
heavenly Father just as you talk with a friend. If
you continue this—reading his guide book, obeying
his instruction, and talking to him—he will also become *you*r life and *your* love. The following poem
depicts my life before and after I accepted the Lord
Jesus:

MY MASTER'S FACE

I had walked life's way with an easy tread,
Had followed where comforts and pleasures led,
Until one day in a quiet place
I met the Master face to face.

With station and wealth and rank for my goal,
Much thought for my body but none for my soul,
I had entered to win in life's mad race,
When I met the Master face to face.

I met him and knew him and blushed to see
That his eyes full of sorrow were fixed on me.
And I faltered and fell at his feet that day
While my castles melted and vanished away.

Melted and vanished, and in their place
Naught else did I see, but the Master's face,
And I cried aloud, "Oh, make me meet
To follow the steps of thy wounded feet."

My thought is now for the souls of men;
I have lost my life to find it again,
E'er since one day in a quiet place
I met the Master face to face.

—Author Unknown

Chapter II

PARTY!

"With God all things are possible"
—Matthew 19:26

Six candles on the red cake! I couldn't believe my eyes. I counted again. My eyes had not deceived me; there were six candles. I stood quietly gazing at the cake and candles. "What does all of this mean, Lord?" I asked. "Are you trying to tell me something?" (I never cease to be amazed how God works both in natural and in supernatural ways his wonders to perform.)

It all began with a phone call. The chairman of the Christian Women's Club in Lansing, Michigan, was calling asking me to speak to her club. I had that date open and accepted. Just before we completed our conversation, she said, "Please don't forget that date." I replied, "Oh, I couldn't; that is my birthday." This portion of the conversation was immediately forgotten by me.

During the past seven years, because of a promise made to God, I have given a brief resumé of our older daughter's life in every speaking engagement. Becky was sixteen when she went to be with our Lord. She was spiritually mature beyond her age. God's grace was outstanding during her illness and

23

death. Sharing it with others has brought many people to a personal encounter with the Lord Jesus Christ. My talk in Lansing was no different in this respect. I closed with the story of our Becky, emphasizing God's wonderful grace available to anyone who will ask for it. Jesus says, "My grace is sufficient for thee" (2 Cor. 12:9).

After the meeting the chairman handed me a box. She said, "Betsy, here is a birthday cake I baked for you. You'll never guess what kind it is." The yummy-looking white frosting hid her secret from me. I said, "No, I *don't* know." She replied, "It's a red cake, have you ever tasted one?" Chills enveloped me. The words didn't come easily. "I just can't believe it. That was Becky's favorite cake." As I peeked into the box again, I noticed some candles on the cake, but I didn't notice the number.

On the return trip I couldn't get *that* cake off my mind. When I arrived home, I told my husband about it. Tears came to his eyes. He followed me into the kitchen and watched as I took the cake from the box. It was then I saw the six candles. Since I see God in every detail of my life, I sensed this was no coincidence. This was a God incident! It would be exactly six years in October since Becky had died.

Silently gazing at the cake and candles, I heard his still small voice. "I want you to give a party as a memorial to Becky." As I continued to listen, he unfolded every detail of the party. It was to be held in our Rescue Mission Auxiliary Room. It was to be given in October, the month Becky left earth to be with him. It was to be one of our regular auxiliary luncheon meetings but I was to be responsible for all the expenses incurred. The two hundred guests were to be seated at card tables covered with lun-

cheon cloths. Gracing the center of each table was
to be a vase of pink rosebuds (Becky's favorite
flower). I was also to donate a memorial gift of two
hundred dollars to a bus fund, our auxiliary project.
(The bus was to be used to pick up children from
all over the city for Sunday school.)

"But, Lord," I questioned, "where will all this
money come from?" Immediately I knew I would
only have to trust him and he would provide, and
he did! Through surprise love offerings from
churches where I spoke, he supplied all the money.
The luncheon menu God gave me was simple but
delicious. I was to serve chicken salad on lettuce,
blueberry muffins, and raspberry nut sherbet. The
Lord followed our usual luncheon routine by supplying a tremendous speaker who spoke on heaven.
The special music was both spiritual and humorous,
two ingredients which were dominant in our Becky's
life.

When the Lord stopped speaking to me, I was astounded that I could receive so many instructions
from him in such a short time. I hurried to the
phone and called the executive director of our auxiliary. I quickly told her all the plans the Lord had
in mind for us. I waited with baited breath when I
told her the party was to be in October. I knew in
previous years we had always omitted a meeting in
October. God again had gone before me and cleared
the way. She said, "No problem. I decided that this
year we are going to have a meeting in October."

God made the preparations for the party exciting
by sprinkling little miracles here and there—like
the evening before the big event. The director and
some of the men at the mission were helping us set
up the card tables and chairs. They kept saying,
"You women can't get two hundred people in

here." We laughed and continued our work. When we finished we had fifty card tables, with four chairs to each, arranged beautifully in the room. They looked at the arrangement and shook their heads. They had forgotten for a moment there is power in prayer. The executive board had prayed with me about each detail of the party.

When the women of the auxiliary heard about the party, I had all kinds of volunteer help. The chicken salad was made in our kitchen. Four women worked at one time for one to two hours. Our sixteen-year-old daughter, Angie, observing this said, "Mother, I can't believe this. You have women working in shifts preparing the chicken salad." This was true, and I hadn't planned it.

On the day of the meeting, our president said, "Betsy doesn't know anything about this. I just have to share the miracle of the raspberry nut sherbet." Our president had ordered the sherbet a month in advance. The day before the meeting she went to the store to pick it up. She was told they were out of raspberry nut sherbet. "But," she lamented, "I ordered it a month ago." "I know," the clerk stated, "but we are all out of it." "What kind do you have?" she asked. "Orange, lime, and rainbow." She thought a moment. "I'll take rainbow. It won't go along with our decor but there is nothing else I can do now."

They loaded nine gallons of the sherbet into the trunk of her car. Dejectedly she walked to her car talking to the Lord all the way. "Lord, you know Betsy wanted raspberry nut sherbet. That's what you told her to have." While driving from the parking lot, she suddenly heard a man calling to her. "Lady, are you the one who wanted nine gallons of raspberry nut sherbet?" "Yes, I am," she called back. He said, "It just came in about five minutes ago. Do you want me to load it into your car?" "Oh, yes, please do, but you have nine gallons of rainbow to unload first." Everyone agreed it was one of God's miracles.

What did God accomplish through this party? Our speaker, at the completion of her talk, asked if there were any who would like to accept Jesus as their Lord and Savior. One soul was ushered into the kingdom of heaven. She also erased all our fear of death when she said, "If God were to let us see heaven now, we couldn't bear to go on living on this earth!" The party also encouraged the women to give their money for the purchase of the bus which is now a reality at the mission. Many of the women said it was the most exciting party they had ever attended.

As the women were leaving the mission, my heart was truly rejoicing in the Lord. I breathed a "Thank you, Lord, nothing is impossible with you." Every detail of this party was planned and executed by our Lord—my life and my love.

Party!

It was an unusual party I will admit
But every detail of it was made to fit.
Into the Rescue Mission Auxiliary's regular meeting
And each person attending was given a special greeting,
Four at a table with a pink rosebud gracing the center.
"My, what beauty," the women exclaimed as they entered.

The room, electrified by God's Holy Spirit,
Each detail given by him was obeyed to the minute.
It was a memorial party for Becky, our daughter
    who is with the Lord,
But for me it was an extra special reward—
To *hear* the women sing, pray, and express love for
    their friends.
The Minnick sisters gave us humor, glorious songs,
    but that wasn't the end.
We had a peek into heaven by Carol Seaman's spe-
    cial talk.
It challenged each one of us to a more holy walk
With Jesus, who had planned this entire affair.
Oh, what a party, because God was there!

—Charlotte Gerig

Chapter III

BECKY

Many lives have been touched by our Becky. Though she is in heaven with the Lord, her witness goes on. Several people have asked why I don't write a book entirely about Becky. The answer is simple. The Lord has not led me to do that. However, he has impressed me that a chapter in this book should share a little more of her personal life with you readers.

While looking through some papers, I found a copy of a letter and a playlet Becky had written. Instead of sharing *my* thoughts about Becky with you, I believe the Lord wants me to share these.

Becky was just a child when she wrote this playlet. It was written at Thanksgiving time for her English class.

The Unthankful Angel

Corinthius (the first angel): People are so unthoughtful. Look at them, Marcellus, they are stuffing themselves with turkey and cranberry sauce. Many of them didn't stop to thank God before they ate. I don't see why he doesn't give up on them.

Marcellus (second angel): Because, Corinthius, God promisèd he wouldn't; besides, there are some who are grateful.

Corinthius: Yes, but just think of the mess they would be in if they didn't have us around to guard them and keep them out of trouble.

Marcellus: This is our job, and it should be a privilege.

Corinthius: Why Marcellus, what have they ever done for us?

Marcellus: Corinthius, are you trying to protect your creator or yourself? Think of him. He never tires of them. He loves them; he wants them to be more like him. He died for them; he paid a price for them. He has given us the greatest gift of all. He has given us the responsibility of taking care of them and to keep them safely. We are God's helpers; we should be thankful. Look at our home. It is beautiful. We can have anything we desire if we only ask him. We not only live well—we know him. There have been many times when I have wanted to shout his glory to all of them down on earth. But he says they must choose and learn for themselves.

Corinthius: Why don't they all love him? Why do they turn their backs on him. Why don't they confess their sins and trust him?

Marcellus: Corinthius, don't you see why? Their eyes are blinded by worldly objects and desires. We should be thankful we already know him.

Corinthius: Again you are right, Marcellus. I have been foolish. Every day should be a Thanksgiving day. Everyone ought always to be thankful—especially us.

Marcellus: God is great and generous. His love is overflowing and endless. Corinthius, let us go to the gates and praise him.

Following is a letter Becky wrote to a young man
at the Interlochen Arts Academy during her junior
year of high school. She had been with him in a
church service in Traverse City, Michigan, when he
made his decision to accept Christ as his Lord and
Savior. Becky accompanied him to the altar. She
had written a rough draft of the letter and copied
it—the reason for my finding the original. I will
share just parts of it. I believe it proves how spiritually mature our teen-agers can be. I believe we do
not encourage our Christian teen-agers enough. We
don't hear enough about them! In the news media
it's always the bad that is magnified. Perhaps we
Christian parents are at fault. Maybe we take our
Christian teen-agers too much for granted. I
changed the name of the young man for obvious
reasons.

"Dear Jeff,
For the past few weeks you have been deep in my
thoughts and a real burden to my heart. My recent
trip to Interlochen intensified this burden to a
greater degree than ever before. I guess in a way
I'm admitting and informing you of the guilt feel-
ings that have been gnawing at my conscience. I
felt led to write to you, not only because I wanted
to but because I feel it my spiritual duty and obli-
gation to my Lord.
Last weekend when I saw you, I sensed you had
some kind of problem but I was unable to draw it
out of you. I thought possibly talking to you would
help in some way but the results, in my opinion,
were quite unsuccessful. Last spring when you accepted Christ I was bound and determined I would
help you in your new life and decision. I wanted to
help as much as possible and in any way I could.

However, I became very busy with my studies and my music. My true responsibility to you and my Lord was somewhat neglected. I'm not making excuses for myself. I have remembered you in prayer daily. But I would like to ask forgiveness from you and offer my aid in any problem you may be experiencing now after having received Christ.

It is so important for you to grow and bloom after receiving Jesus as your Savior. Too many people do not take advantage of the gift of salvation and the personal walk with the Lord. One cannot stop with salvation, or the thrill of his new life will soon dwindle away. He will find his life again burdened with easily avoidable problems.

I hope you won't feel me presumptuous, Jeff, but I *know* Christ is the answer. In my situation I believe I am facing one of the most critical problems of my life or anyone's life—death. I, too, at different periods have experienced confusion to the point of not knowing whether it was all worth it. These times have passed for me. I don't mean that the Christian walk is a bed of roses. But at least we have the complete assurance of sustainment, grace, and help in all our difficulties regardless of what they are.

The one key, Jeff, is faith. We must trust the Lord in all things and completely trust. He created the universe, and because he did this his power is great enough to see the whole picture, thus enabling him to guide and direct all things. It isn't always easy to leave the decisions up to him. It isn't easy to go on trusting him regardless of circumstances. I know, Jeff, all about this because of my own personal experience this past year. Many people at Interlochen, including yourself, knew noth-

ing about the trials that not only I but my family
have endured this past year.

To begin with there was the first surgery, then
the infection and the second surgery. The doctors
than found a recurrence of the tumor. At one time
during all this I began to feel my faith slipping. At
this point I wondered if there really is a Supreme
Being. I talked with our pastor, Mr. Mitchell. I told
him I felt as if I were in the middle of Grand Cen-
tral Station in New York, wandering around with
the lights out, separated completely from Jesus. He
guided me into some study in the Bible. I read the
Bible, searched the Scriptures, and prayed. I found
my Lord again! The doctors told me at Christmas I
had only three months to live. Here I am in August
still alive and as happy as ever.

I know, Jeff, that he is always with us, and regardless of what happens to us he will never leave
us or forsake us. I'm sending you a devotional book
that has helped me in my daily quiet time. Jeff, I
have found that having a set time each day to read
the Bible and my devotional book and to talk to
our Lord is the secret of the Christian walk.

Love in Christ,
Becky"

Living with Becky during the year and half of
her illness ushered me into spiritual rooms in God's
mansion I didn't dream existed. The luxury I've enjoyed in these rooms is pure ecstasy. The following
poem which the Lord gave me for this chapter is a
summary of Becky's life. May it challenge you to
become a believer in the Lord Jesus. If you are a
believer, may this chapter be a stepping stone to
surrender your all to Jesus. Make him *your* life and
your love.

Becky

The day that Becky met Jesus was a day to behold.
In him she found eternal life and it had to be told.
He was also *her* life and her love—
Love she gave to others, from God above.
She left a great heritage to many on this earth—
Her life was radiant with the *truth* and full of mirth.
When God took her to heaven, he replaced our tears with a smile
Because we had the assurance she had run a beautiful race.
She ran into Jesus' arms, all because of his grace.
As a child she had asked his forgiveness and accepted Christ as her friend,
Also as her Savior from sin; we pray her witness will send
You to him. You need no longer hope or wish for eternal life.
Just read and obey John 3:16, there will be no more strife.
You will be a Christian, what glory that will be.
You can shout, "Hallelujah," and be with him throughout eternity.

Chapter IV

SILENCE

"I can do all things through Christ which strengtheneth me."
—Philippians 4:13

"In quietness and in confidence shall be your strength."
—Isaiah 30:15

"She can never do it. No, she'll never be able to do it." It was my husband speaking. We were entertaining Ginnie and Frank Bryan in our living room after having been out to dinner together.

Jack and Frank are like brothers, very close professionally. The four of us are close socially, and attending the same church brings us even closer. Ginnie, Frank, and I have known one another for years. I had just completed my nurse's training when Ginnie entered the program. I was Nursing Arts Instructress on the wards and taught Ginnie the art of filling a hot water bottle, for one thing. If you don't think that is an art, just try lying on one that's filled with too much water. The rest of the bottle is filled with air and looks like a balloon. It also feels as if you're trying to sleep on one. Through this contact Ginnie and I were drawn together. Frank also happened to be working in the same hospital, City Hospital (now General) in Indianapolis, Indiana, where he was a medical student.

I was talking fast and furiously when Jack made that statement, "She'll never be able to do it." I looked at him and said, "Jack, you know you are right. I certainly will not be able to keep silent in my own strength. However, there is a little promise in the Bible that states, 'I can do all things through Christ which strengtheneth me.' I plan to take that promise with me to the hospital and just lean on the Lord and his promise."

At this point in the conversation the Lord gave me the title for this chapter through Frank. After hearing me repeat the Bible verse, Frank said, "Why don't you call one of the chapters in your second book 'There's Strength in Silence.' " I said, "But, Frank, I can't. Each title is to be just one word." He replied, "Okay, then, Just 'Silence'." Thank you, Lord, again for using your servants to help one another. Frank, I dedicate this chapter to you.

Many of my friends gave me encouraging words about having to go into the hospital as a patient. They all helped. The words our secretary, Catherine Miller, said to me were precious. They might comfort you just now. Perhaps you have been laid aside. She said, "Betsy, isn't this a wonderful gift of rest to you from our Lord for all you have done for him?" I hadn't thought of it as a gift at all. In fact I was sad about the whole thing. I was having to ask Donna Kent to take my speaking engagements. Ginnie Bryan was generous and gracious to take my Bible study group. And then all the other things I was doing for the Lord! Giving them all up—a gift from God?

I accepted it! Right then and there it was his gift to me, a gift of rest. My whole attitude changed. It's how we look at things that makes the difference. A verse of scripture has given me a real sense of comfort in those times when the unexpected comes along and tempts me to get ruffled. It came from Ethel Anderson, chairman of Winsome Women. She was speaking to our Christian Women's Club. Take it for your very own and hide it in your heart. "This also cometh forth from the Lord of hosts, which is wonderful in counsel, and excellent in working" (Isa. 28:29).

This is my ninth day in my little room—"Haven of Rest," I call it. It really has been that. A sign on my door says, "No Visitors." Another one put up yesterday says, "Complete voice rest—don't ask the patient any questions." I believe this is one of the strictest disciplinary measures I've ever experienced. Now I have just a slight idea of what one experiences when not being allowed to speak. You should see me having one of my hot moist treatments with a contraption they call a hydrocollar. I look as if I'm about to take off for the moon with the astronauts.

Our sixteen-year-old daughter Angie and her dad are both so busy that their in-and-outs seem like seconds. But then I look at the little plaque Mary Beltz gave me just before I came into the hospital. It says, "In everything give thanks" (1 Thess. 5:18). I pause and give thanks for this cozy little room and all the wonderful cards, flowers, and gifts. I especially give thanks for the love that comes with each one. I've actually felt the love—Christ's love—pouring in to me from everything I have received. He always balances the scales, sending blessings along with the trials. True, I've had times when tears have come and they would probably come in torrents if I had permitted them. But I recognized them as tears of self-pity and would not permit them. Again I would say, "Thank you, Lord, for everything." The precious sisters here at St. Joseph's Hospital come and see me periodically. They call themselves my "immediate family," and they *are* because we are really one in Christ!

God has brought about some very exciting happenings through my first book, *The Valley of Vision*. While I was in the hospital someone was chatting with me about the book. She said, "Have you ever heard of an organization for the blind that records Christian books?" I said, "No, I know nothing about such an organization." She answered quickly, "I do. Wouldn't it be great if your book could be recorded by them?" I agreed and replied how pleased I would be if that could happen. I had no idea how this could ever come about.

After coming home from the hospital, I received the following letter from Dr. Phillips of Warner Press.

"Dear Betsy,

In Minneapolis, Minnesota, there is an organization called the Martha Arney Library for the Blind. It is a tax-exempt, non-profit organization dedicated solely to recording Christian books for use by the blind.

We have given permission to this organization to record *The Valley of Decision* for circulation and use by their organization."

"Before they call, I will answer; and while they are yet speaking, I will hear" (Isa. 65:24).

"Silence is golden." I've pondered about this phrase all my life. I've thought and meditated over it. What does it mean? What could be golden about keeping your mouth shut? What did the word *golden* have to do with being quiet?

I'll admit I've always enjoyed talking. When I was a little girl with my aunt and uncle and cousins, if things got quiet or dull, I would say, "I'll speak a piece." The pieces I spoke were usually "Cleaning Out the Furnace" by Edgar A. Guest, or "Old Mister Moon." And then there was "Betty at the Baseball Game." That one was a real dinger. It had everyone laughing. Some of you probably remember it.

Golden denotes something beautiful—to remain silent before God, listening to what he has to say to us, instead of always doing the talking. There are precious verses in the Bible concerning silence, and since they are beautiful, perhaps we can compare them to gold. "A talebearer revealeth secrets: but he that is of a faithful spirit concealeth the matter" (Prov. 11:13). This is a golden verse. "He that answereth a matter before he heareth it, it is folly and shame unto him" (Prov. 18:13). Keep silent at the right times. "The Lord is in his holy temple: let all the earth keep silence before him" (Hab. 2:20). "Be not rash with thy mouth, and let not thine heart be hasty to utter anything before God: for God is in heaven, and thou upon earth: therefore let thy words be few" (Eccles. 5:2). "A time to keep silence, and a time to speak" (Eccles. 3:7). After reading and meditating on these beautiful scriptures, I have become fully convinced that silence is golden.

There is also great strength in silence. I endured much pain while in the hospital, even with all the medication, but I just looked up and asked Jesus for his strength and he has seen me through each time. He never fails—Jesus, my life and my love.

Silence

Silence is a golden thread
Interwoven around every thought of hope.
If God is with you in it,
You will discover a beautiful rope
Of his lovely pearls,
And you'll find no end to its infinite length.

Remember this: "In quietness and in confidence shall be your strength."

Chapter V

MINIES

"Ah Lord God! behold, thou hast made the heaven and the earth by thy great power and stretched out arm, and there is nothing too hard for thee."

—Jeremiah 32:17

Skirts? Dresses? No, I want to share with you some miracles. Our God is a God of miracles. "Jesus Christ the same yesterday, and today, and for ever" (Heb. 13:81). If God is *your* life and *your* love you should be enjoying an exciting life sprinkled with "mini-miracles."

Please don't misunderstand—I believe and know the greatest of all miracles God performs is changing a person's heart. He changed my heart and I became personally acquainted with him. But since that time he has performed many miracles in my life. In these past six months there has been an abundance of them. Many of my friends have asked me to record them in this book. Here are a few.

The Valley of Vision had just been published. I had a speaking engagement at the Christian Women's Club in Richmond, Indiana. I awakened the morning before with the thought that I needed a new fall outfit for it. My next thought was, I have no car today. I said, "Lord, how do I get to the shopping center if this is what you want me to do?"

Suddenly the phone rang. "How would you like to go shopping today?" asked my friend, Agnes Krick. "Thank you, Lord," I said quietly. "I surely would," I replied. She came and picked me up. You will see from this miracle that God's timing is perfect. Just before we left she said, "Betsy, will you autograph some of your books for me?" "Agnes, let's wait until we get back. We'll have more time." She agreed and we were on our way. She had to stop and get a check cashed. When we arrived at the shopping center (one to which I *never* go for clothing but I had suggested it) she suggested we stop and have a bite to eat. We dawdled over a second cup of coffee.

Finally we went to the store to look for clothes. I tried on dress after dress with no success. Then I found myself looking at things I wasn't interested in, taking up still more time. As we were walking out the door, I told Agnes I was disappointed. Before we had left the house we had prayed that the Lord would direct us to the store of his choice. "Agnes, we obeyed but here I am without anything!" By this time we were out of the store and walking down the sidewalk. Agnes said, "Betsy, would you like to go someplace else and look?" I said, "No, by the time we go to the grocery, get home, and *I autograph* your books, I will have had it for the day."

Just then a young man approached me from the side. He spoke very excitedly. "Are you Mrs. Patterson?" I said, "Yes, I am. How did you know?" He explained by relating the following story.

That morning he had been to a drugstore near my husband's office. He had talked with the pharmacist, Bill Byrum, a friend of ours. During the conversation he asked Bill if he knew of any newly published books. Bill told him about *The Valley of Vision*. The young man asked him where he could purchase it. Bill directed him to the Gospel Temple Book Store in the southeast part of town. He went to the bookstore and bought one.

On his way home (he lived in a town north of Fort Wayne) he decided he would call me. He explained further that he represented the Successful Living Company. This company places books on racks in airports, drugstores, and so forth all over the country. He stated he wanted to contact me to see how he could purchase *The Valley of Vision* for his company. As he was driving along he remembered that the only *outside* phone easily accessible was in a shopping center. It was the same shopping area in which Agnes and I were. Incidentally, this shopping area took him back across town to the northwest corner once again. He explained, "I was walking to the phone behind the two of you when I heard you say, '*autograph your books*.' The Holy Spirit whispered into my ear, 'You don't need to phone her—there she is.'" God's split-second timing! We stood there stunned. He promised he would pray for great sales of the book. I thanked him and we left each other.

The next day on my way to Richmond to my speaking engagement, I stopped to see Dr. Phillips of Warner Press. I told him this story. When I finished he said, "Betsy, we have already sent the Successful Living Company one of your books. We are now waiting to hear from them." The next morning Dr. Phillips called me and said that the Successful Living Company had just called and ordered five thousand books. I was ecstatic. Had the young man had anything to do with it? I decided to call him. He said he hadn't contacted the company, but he had just mailed the book to them. I said, "Why do you suppose God permitted the miracle at the shopping center?" He said, "I've shared it with lots of people." I replied, "I have too." He continued to say he was going to reveal the miracle at a sales meeting which would include salesmen from all over the United States. *"That* should sell the book." God truly is a God of miracles. He had each of us in the exact spot and permitted that young man to hear me say "autograph your books" at the right moment.

Again the Lord proved to me he is interested in every detail of our lives. He showed me in another fascinating way that he wanted to be my business partner. I was helping out with the secretarial duties at our office while our secretary was on vacation. We receive many advertisements in the mail. One day I was sorting it. I had the last letter in my hand. In essence it said one could buy a number of pens and receive the same number free. I thought, why would they send my husband such an advertisement? What would he do with five hundred or a thousand ballpoint pens? I had my hand in the waste basket. Then I put the letter back on my desk to read it more thoroughly. It stated that one might have an inscription printed on the pen. I wrote with the sample pen and found it to be very good.

I picked it up and looked at it again. I could see (in my mind's eye) printed across it, "Read *The Valley of Vision* by Betsy Patterson." "Oh you wouldn't, Lord," I said aloud. "Would you permit me to advertise your book this way?" I was impressed with a "yes." When my husband came in I explained the plan to him. I would buy the pens and give them to the different bookstores to hand out. I would also give them to our friends. He thought it was a great plan. So did the bookstores *and* my friends. I also checked with Dr. Phillips. He approved. Through the grapevine I've heard many books have sold through the pens. Praise the Lord!

Here is another double "mini" I think you will enjoy. These are small things but, oh so precious—at least to me.

My brother Paul and his wife Mary Lou were visiting us from Texas. It was the week of my first autograph party for *The Valley of Vision*. I was extremely happy to have them at the party because one of the chapters in the book is dedicated to Paul. Did they just *happen* to be visiting us? No, it was another *God incident*.

During the week they were with us I had a speaking engagement at a church. Mary Lou accompanied me. I had my hair styled with a screw-type curl in front of each ear. As we were nearing our destination, Mary Lou said, "Betsy, one of your curls is longer than the other. It doesn't look right. Do you have a pair of scissors in your purse?" Of course, I didn't. She continued to talk about that curl. In the meantime my thoughts were on the books I had with us to sell to anyone who desired one. After the book was published, my husband and I had decided there would be no money exchanged inside a church for the book. I took a box of books along on faith, telling the Lord I didn't know how he was going to take care of them. I said I would be willing to sell them in the parking lot if that's what he wanted.

Mary Lou continued to complain about my curl as we entered the church. After our greetings I asked several of the women if we might have prayer together for the entire meeting. They led us into a tiny hall. It was very narrow but up against the wall was an old desk. Mary Lou immediately began to open the drawers. I said, "What are you looking for?" She replied, "A pair of scissors." I said, "Oh, forget the curl and let's pray." After we prayed, I opened one of the drawers, shuffled a few papers around, and found, peeking up at me, a pair of tiny scissors. "Praise the Lord," Mary Lou said. "I prayed there would be a pair of scissors in that desk." She cut the curl to match the other one and was happy. "But the very hairs of your head are all numbered" (Matt. 10:30).

The women were all gathered together in the church sanctuary. I assumed the entire meeting, including the banquet, would be held in the church. I was thinking we would have to sell the books in the parking lot. The next thing I knew the chairman was leading us outside the church. She began apologizing because we were going to have to walk a few yards over to a school building where they were going to hold the banquet. It was my turn to praise the Lord. Now we could sell the books in the building!

They prepared a table on which to put the books. Just before leaving home I grabbed up a bunch of pens imprinted with the name of the book and put them in the box with the books. I told the chairman I planned to give one with each book sold. She said, "Wouldn't it be nice to put one at each person's plate as a favor?" We all agreed. I looked at them. Would there be enough? Before I could say a word, Mary Lou was off and putting one at each place. I reminded her not to put one at our places as we had plenty at home. While I was arranging the books, she came to me and said, "Betsy, *can you believe* I have one for each place but one?" I said, "Mary Lou, *can you believe* the Lord had me pick up one at the last minute and put it in my purse?" Fresh mini-miracles out of God's kingdom of miracles to share with these dear women!

I have people say to me, "Can these miracles happen to anyone?" My answer is "Yes, they can." For example, I was with Fran Dickinson on a tour of the Holy Land. Since it was near Christmas, she planned to send her Christmas cards from the Holy Land. After arriving in the Holy Land she discovered she had left her list of names and addresses at home. She was really upset. "How could I have done such a thing?" she said. We were staying at the King George Hotel in Jerusalem. Fran and I were roommates. I was planning to call Emil and Waddad Abu Dayeh, my friends in Jerusalem. After we were settled in our hotel room, I began to look for the telephone directory. Fran was helping me. We were opening first one drawer and then another. "I can't believe it, I can't believe it," Fran practically shouted. "What are you talking about?" I said. "Come over here and look, Betsy." I looked in the drawer. Guess what we saw! There lay a Fort Wayne, Indiana, phone directory! God takes care of his own.

Donna Kent related another miraculous story to me and I am quoting it as follows in her own words:

"There is that urgency and knowledge that God has a task for you to do but you are not quite certain how it will be accomplished. This was the way Wilf and I felt when we agreed to go as a team for four days to Rochester, New York. What would we do with our four children? How would we explain to them our absence? Could they accept being left and not feel resentment over the fact that mom and dad were going to minister to others? As a mother I particularly felt this burden. But as I sought for someone to care for them, I felt no peace. No one could be found to stay with them. I considered not going, but again there was that urgency: 'I have a task for you to do.'

"Finally I rested my case in the Lord and asked no one to care for the children. When my husband asked me if arrangements were made, I simply said I wasn't sure. I reminded the Lord he had called us to serve and we were willing. He would have to meet the need of our four precious children. Since time was running out I could not understand the peace I felt, but then one day I knew.

"The pastor of the church which had invited us came to Fort Wayne for a mission board meeting. We entertained him and his family in our home and as the evening drew to a close he said, 'I feel led to tell you to bring your children with you. We will give you adequate accommodations. You pay for your children's expenses and we will take care of you and your husband.'

"I was quick to recognize a problem. 'I cannot speak and care for the children also. I must have some quietness.' 'No problem,' the pastor quickly assured me. 'There are lots of winter sports (which, by the way, the children enjoy very much) and we will see that they are entertained and taken care of while you are there.'

"That night I wept tears of joy and thanksgiving as I recalled our excitement as we told our children what God had arranged for them. You say coincidence—not a chance! Our heavenly Father knows our needs and desires. He wants to have a part in every aspect of our lives. The answer came when I stooped fretting and left the details in his all-knowing hands."

A lovely couple, Larry and Ellen Chrouch, are avid believers that prayer changes things. They also are constantly looking for mini-miracles. About three years ago Larry's work transferred him from Cincinnati to Huron, Ohio. They prayed together about selling their home. They discussed the situation. Should they try to sell it themselves or put it in the hands of a real estate agent? Before they had the opportunity to do either, a couple came to their door and asked them if they would be willing or interested in selling their house. To them this was a mini-miracle!

I just had a note from Ellen telling me of a new job Larry now has back in Cincinnati. They put their home up for sale. The first couple that looked at their home bought it. Praise the Lord!

Another mini-miracle happened to me one morning. Circumstances had come about that brought a desperate need for me to have our home cleaned that day. I called my dear friend Esther Hermann (she also cleans our home) to see if she could come right away.

She said she didn't think she could as she had made a promise to another woman for that day. However, she said she would call her and see what arrangements could be made. Esther sounded very dubious about being able to come here. I prayed about it and began to read the Bible. At once this verse popped out at me. "For he shall deliver the needy when he crieth; the poor also, and him that hath no helper" (Ps. 72:12). I said, "Lord, I believe this promise." Within seconds Esther called me back and said she could come. A coincidence or luck? No, a mini-miracle!

Driving home from my husband's office one afternoon, I felt weary and a little "down." "Lord," I said, "if I could only hear from someone for whom I have prayed to know you have answered their need. I need some encouragement, Lord." That prayer was answered almost immediately. I stopped at the mailbox before driving into the garage and found a letter from Mil Bucher from Valparaiso. I had met her only once when I spoke at the Christian Women's Club there. At that time she gave me a prayer request. Now she was writing to tell me of our answered prayer! Mini-miracles strengthen our faith.

I always pray about parking places for my car, don't you? I was at the beauty shop. Bonnie Smith was doing my hair. Bonnie's ministry is praying for others. She is truly faithful to her calling. She asked me if I could stay a few minutes and pray with another patron of hers. Isn't it fabulous to think prayer can be said for others *even* in a beauty shop? I was due at the Rescue Mission Women's Auxiliary luncheon but said that of course I would be glad to pray with her. On the way to the Mission I said, "You know, Lord, I'm late. You know how many cars are already parked there. Please save a place for me. Thank you." When I turned into the drive at the Mission the Lord had saved the very first spot for me. He also had a man standing there to direct me into the spot. "If ye abide in me, and my words abide in you, ye shall ask what ye will, and it shall be done unto you" (John 15:7).

Last night I was speaking to my husband from this beautiful spot on Hilton Head Island. I was lamenting that with all the beauty around me I was lonely. He sympathized with me and reminded me it would be only a couple of days before I would be home. This morning the Lord had something to say to me through one of my devotional books. The Lord hears everything! "God has chosen the best place in which you can do your best work. Perhaps you may be lonely but you have no right to complain. The Master has put you here and it is enough being in his will." I asked God's forgiveness for being lonely and thanked him for all the beauty around me. How can we *doubt* our God is concerned with the tiny details of our lives? "Let all those that seek thee rejoice and be glad in thee: and let such as love thy salvation say continually, Let God be magnified" (Ps. 70:4). The most I can do is give praise to our Lord Jesus—my life and my love.

Minies

I call them minies, the tiny miracles that come
from God's hand.
If you do not know Jesus personally you will not
understand—
It's the little things I see him in, that are very precious to me.
Many do not notice them because they are not
looking, you see.
Put God into *every* detail—put him first in everything.
Then you'll see minies in your life which cause your
heart to sing.

Chapter VI

SOCIALITES

"And whosoever was not found written in the book of life was cast into the lake of fire."

—Revelation 20:15

Is your name written in God's book of life? If so, you are definitely on God's society page.

All of us at some time in our lives, in our humanness, desired to be noticed publicly. Perhaps you had this desire in grade school, high school, college, or in business. Some men and women have an insatiable desire for prestige—to be accepted by men regardless of the consequences. They are willing to risk being criticized and even hated if they can be in the limelight constantly.

The exciting way to become a socialite is knowing God through his Son Jesus Christ. "I am the way, the truth, and the life: no man cometh unto the Father, but by me" (John 14:6). Jesus said that! When you are a Christian you are honored, revered, and blessed throughout eternity by the heavenly Father.

I had read Revelation 20:15 many times. It never came alive to me until I had this experience. I was invited by Mary Ann Beltz to accompany her on a speaking engagement. We were enjoying refreshments after the program. Suddenly the woman sitting beside me exclaimed, "I wonder if you could give me some words of encouragement. I have accepted the chairmanship of our mother-daughter banquet. I have never done anything like this before. I'm scared to death." A scripture verse immediately came to my mind. "I have a promise from the Bible I'll give you." She quickly wrote it on a scrap of paper and put it in her purse. It was Philippians 4:13. "I can do all things through Christ which strengtheneth me."

Some Christians do not bother to memorize scriptures. I believe God's Word has supernatural power. We should memorize verses from the Bible. The Holy Spirit can then bring them to our minds when we need them. In Psalm 119:11 we read, "Thy word have I hid in mine heart, that I might not sin against thee." He wants us to know what is in the handbook he has given to us as a guide for living. This woman promised she would trust the Lord and rely on the promise I had given to her.

Soon after this incident a young woman called me to speak to her mother-daughter banquet. I accepted. In the course of the conversation she said, "Mrs. Abner Gerig is the chairman of the affair." I immediately recognized the name as that of the woman to whom I had given the verse.

A couple of days later I received a large envelope. In it was a short note attached to a sizeable number of poems. The note asked if I would read each poem and choose the one I thought the best. She added the poems were written by the daughters of their church about their mothers. Never before had I been a judge of anything. *I* couldn't choose the best one. But the Lord could. I asked the Lord to choose the one he believed to be the best.

The night of the banquet they called on me to read the poem I had chosen. I explained to the group that I had asked the Lord to do the choosing. I read the poem and to my utter amazement it had been written by the chairman's daughter. As Mrs. Gerig stood for her applause, I could sense she was somewhat embarrassed but she was also very excited and happy.

Two or three nights later her daughter called to say her mother was in the hospital with a malignant brain tumor. She asked me to pray for her. Many of us prayed. The Lord chose to take her home to be with him.

The Lord never makes a mistake! He gave his precious daughter, Mrs. Gerig, a beautiful honor at her last social function. Her daughter talked with me several times about her mother. I knew from our conversations that her mother's name was certainly written in God's book of life.

I'm closing this chapter with the poem I read at that special mother-daughter banquet.

I'm including it as a memorial to Mrs. Abner Gerig and to my own mother who is with the Lord. Jesus was their life and their love!

Society Page Women

Society page women
Are very special, you know—
Such women are few
The percentage is low.

But even more special—
And rare in this age—
Are those very few women
Who make God's society page.

And I'm proud to say
That I *know* one of these,
She is not just an acquaintance—
But my mother, you see.

She's adorned with meekness
And quietness, too.
God calls these the ornaments
Of beauty, that's true.

Her credentials are service
To family and friend.
Often *self* she puts last,
Looking out for my end.

And first on the list
Is her top quality:
That of love—first to God
And then family.

Now, dear mother,
Accept these, the praises you've earned,
With a prayer that all you have given
May two-fold be returned.

And, dear God, I'm so thankful
That in this day and age
You have blessed me with a mother
Who's on your society page.

—Charlotte Gerig

Chapter VII

TEEN-AGERS

"Wow, what a dream! I glanced at the clock and it said 2:00 A.M. I was wide awake. Part of this chapter was written during the Christmas holidays of 1972. I am now finishing it on the beach at Hilton Head over a year later. The dream had been terrible. It was about our sixteen-year-old daughter Angie. Immediately the desire came to me to jump from my bed and run to her room. Is she all right? I thought. Sandy, a dear friend of Angie's, was spending the night with us. How could I knock on the door in the middle of the night and say, "Are you all right, Angie?" I thought about the details of the dream. Fear reared its ugly head again. I began to shake all over. I thought, This is ridiculous. I dreamed that dream because of all those little goodies and tidbits I had eaten earlier that evening. Of course, that's why I dreamed this dream.

I quietly slipped out of bed into the bathroom. I sat down on our vanity bench. There it was again—that terrible dream. Angie—was she all right? I began to pray the Twenty-Third Psalm. As I was praying, the word "teen-agers" came to my mind; I couldn't shake it. It was then I knew the Lord had awakened me from this dream to give me the title to this chapter. He also began to put together some of the thoughts Angie and I had talked about during the past few days. This was the second night Sandy had spent with us. The three of us had conversed about many subjects: boys (naturally), clothes, dating, and mothers. Along with these we discussed the subject of courtesy. In face, we started with that and it led to the others.

I would like to share with you a few of the girls' thoughts about courtesies girls should extend to their dates. Girls desire little courtesies themselves, such as having a chair pulled back for them when they are eating out, having the car door opened for them, and receiving compliments on their clothes. If girls desire this, don't boys desire courtesies also? Perhaps complimenting him on how sharp he looks or thanking him for the hamburger and Coke. ("It just hit the spot.") Perhaps he had spent a considerable sum of money on her—an extra "thank you" is in order.

Back to the dream. The Lord permitted it for a purpose. He wanted me to consider the ultimatums I had issued to Angie in the past few days. Were they *his* ultimatums or were they mine? I'm going to share the dream with you because it may give you some insight into your actions and words with your teen-agers. I saw Angie committing suicide, stabbing herself to death. As I prayed and meditated about the dream, I saw it did have definite meaning for me. I had been criticizing her often in small things—things that really didn't matter when I stopped to think about them. To Angie they loomed up as *big* things. She took each criticism seriously and stabbed herself with it which in turn made her feel a deep sense of guilt within. I talked with Angie about this. I told her I had been hasty in my remarks and had said things without thinking.

Angie is a Christian. We guide and direct her but I do not believe it is our duty to convict her. The Holy Spirit will do the convicting. For instance, she wanted to get her ears pierced. I said a flat "no." I didn't even think it through. She said, "Mother, the Lord hasn't convicted me about having it done and you know the Bible says that the Lord looks on the heart, not on the outward appearance." What could I say to that?

If Christian teen-agers find that things are not going well for them, perhaps they need to examine themselves. Are they obeying their parents? The Bible says, "Children, obey your parents in all things: for this is well pleasing unto the Lord" (Col. 3:20). Perhaps they are not having their daily quiet time (reading the Bible and talking with the Lord).

The Scriptures say we should give thanks in all things (1 Thess. 5:18).

Angie and I have had two experiences with this scripture. We were driving home one afternoon. The streets were very icy. She suggested we go a different way as she thought it faster. I objected, but gave in to her wishes. Suddenly the car began sliding. Traffic was coming toward us and from behind us. All drivers stopped and waited to see what was going to happen to us. We finally stopped. We easily could have gone into a ditch. We were in the opposite lane going the opposite direction. Angie said, "Mother, do you know you were saying, 'Thank you Jesus, thank you Jesus,' all the time we were sliding?"

The other experience that stands out in my mind is the time we thanked God for a "D" Angie re-

ceived on her report card. We were planning a trip
to San Antonio to attend our older son's commis-
sioning service in the Air Force. We were driving
and leaving on Monday. My husband told Angie if
she didn't get any grade below a "C" on her report
card he would talk with the principal and ask to
have her excused for the week. You can imagine the
sadness in her heart when she found a "D" on her
report card. She knew she wouldn't be able to go
with us. I said, "The Bible says to give thanks in all
things. Angie, let's thank God for this 'D.'" We
went back to our bedroom. With tears streaming
down our faces and sobs in our throats, we held
hands and praised and thanked God for the "D."
We also praised and thanked him that she would
not be able to go on the trip. It was very difficult
for her. My mother heart was breaking as I
thanked God for this. Each day we continued to
thank him.

Several days before we were to leave, my husband took Angie to school as usual. From school he
normally went on to make his hospital rounds, but
that morning he came back to the house. I said,
"Honey, what are you doing back here?" He replied, "I just came back to tell you that I'm going
to surprise Angie." "What do you mean," I asked.
"Oh, I'm going out to the airport and pick up a
ticket for her. She can fly down to San Antonio on
Thursday with Betty Whiting." (Betty is the
mother-in-law of our younger son, Mort.) I was ecstatic. As it turned out, a close friend, Agnes Krick,
took Angie to get a few new clothes for the celebra-
tion. Angie and Betty had a great time on the plane
trip down. The most beautiful part was that Angie
and I were again impressed and rejoicing in the love
of our heavenly Father. He does hear prayers of

thanksgiving and praise. He does answer. "Giving thanks always for all things unto God and the Father in the name of our Lord Jesus Christ" (Eph. 5:20).

For many years I have meditated over the verse, "By him therefore let us offer the sacrifice of praise to God continually, that is, the fruit of our lips giving thanks to his name" (Heb. 13:15).

I wondered what was meant by the phrase "sacrifice of praise." One day as I was reading it I was enlightened. We are continually wanting to ask God for something. It's difficult in our praying to pray a few sentences without presenting a petition. So when we just praise and do not ask, we are sacrificing our asking for praise. Why didn't I see it before? Have you tried not to ask God for a thing for one whole day? Just thank and praise him the entire day? Try it. It isn't easy. You will find it to be a sacrifice.

In my opinion there is no "generation gap" between teen-agers and adults. I believe that phrase was started by someone a few years ago as an ugly rumor. If you tell someone he is being mistreated by another every hour on the hour, he's going to begin to believe it. Right? Many teen-agers, as well as adults, have come to believe this ugly rumor. Some adults are afraid of teen-agers. Teen-agers aren't afraid of adults. I believe they want to talk with us and get our opinions.

For example, Angie had a letter from a friend, Clark Shaughnessey, some months ago. He had been in our home numerous times but I had never had the opportunity to talk with him any more than just a friendly greeting. I did not think he would ever give our family a second thought. At the end of his letter he said, "I hope your family is

okay and tell your mother I said hello. Tell her
she's doing a fine job of raising you. I enjoyed
hearing her voice for one minute. [He had called
to talk to Angie during Thanksgiving vacation.]
Tell her to give me some words of wisdom. Seriously!"

Clark, I haven't seen you to talk with you. This
morning I asked the Lord what he had to say to
teen-agers. I have *no* wisdom of my own, only what
the Lord has given to me. "The fear of the Lord is
the beginning of knowledge: but fools despise wisdom and instruction. My son, hear the instruction
of thy father, and forsake not the law of thy mother: for they shall be an ornament of grace unto thy
head, and chains about thy neck. My son, if sinners
entice thee, consent thou not" (Prov. 1:7-10).

"The fear of the Lord is the beginning of knowledge." To me this means that when we accept Jesus
Christ as our personal Savior, he becomes our
friend and then we begin to have knowledge. We
begin to learn the *truth* that sets us free. God
through Jesus Christ is the *only* way. "There is a
way which seemeth right unto a man, but the end
thereof are the ways of death" (Prov. 14:12).

I have a chapter on the rearing of children in my
first book. I do not wish to repeat it here. Remember, mothers and dads, if you rear your children in the knowledge and admonition of the Lord,
you become free when it comes time for them to
leave the nest. You have obeyed the Lord and they
are now his responsibility.

God answers prayers for all who believe—not
hope—he will answer. It was through prayer that a
darling young woman, Sandy Cheever, came into
our lives. Angie and I prayed that God would send
Angie a true friend. One evening Sandy came home

from school with her. Immediately I knew she was the answer to our prayers. Thank you for Sandy, Lord. Since Angie and I talk much about the Lord, Sandy took it all in. Angie shared her devotional books and I shared verses from the Bible with Sandy. We prayed together. One noon Angie called me. Her voice was filled with joy. She said, "Mom, Sandy wants to talk with you." Sandy came on the line. She said, "I was walking here on the grounds of the school and I asked the Lord to come into my heart and life." I knew all the angels of heaven were shouting and rejoicing over Sandy's decision.

One afternoon Sandy called me (her mother was out of town). She was crying. She was finishing a dress she had to wear that night in a concert. She had a very short time in which to finish it. She said she just could not get those puff sleeves in properly and she also had the hem to put in yet. I told her to go back to the dress and I would pray for her. I did. God cares for his own. Sandy was at the concert on time. Angie said Sandy's dress looked beautiful.

Teen-agers do respect their elders and love them if their elders are worthy of their respect and love them in return. Our Rescue Mission Women's Auxiliary was having its monthly luncheon. I was called to the phone. Angie and Sandy were talking to me, first one, then the other, asking if we would have all the women at the auxiliary pray for a problem of a certain friend of theirs. The women were flattered to think teen-agers would want their prayers.

Ann and Lou Schneider are precious friends of ours. They have known us for years and watched our children grow up. Our children have always loved Lou and Ann. It is very apparent the love is returned. For about eight years they had been with us for Christmas dinner. Angie said this year, "It

just won't be Christmas without the Schneiders."
Angie was delighted when they gave her a wooden
Japanese doll as a gift this Christmas. We didn't
realize they knew Angie collected wooden dolls
from different countries. During the holidays they
invited her and a group of her friends over one evening. The Schneiders are world travelers and they
showed the teen-agers their collections from all
over the world. Those kids loved it. They also enjoyed Ann's delicious dainties for refreshment.
Generation gap? If there is, it's of our making. Perhaps we need to look back over our lives and see
where we have failed.

A significant incident happened last Christmas.
Sandy gave Jack and me a beautiful handblown
glass well. It sits in a prominent place in our living
room and is a conversation piece. Betty Ross visited me one day and I showed it to her. She said,
"It's symbolic of the well of living waters that Jesus
talked about." It truly is and we have accepted
it as such.

I want to close this chapter with Bev Brun's
story. She came home from school with Angie and
Sandy one afternoon. The kids perched themselves
up on the counter and began to talk. I didn't leave
the room but began talking with them. One thing
led to another and at some place in the conversation I said something about the "quiet time." Bev
said, "What is that?" I explained and before she
left, since she was all ears, I gave her my book that
had just been published. A week or so later Bev
pulled Angie and Sandy aside in school and told
them about this beautiful experience.

"Before this experience with the Lord happened,
I feel he was preparing me for it in many different
ways.

"Things weren't going too well for me, and as a result I fell back on the Bible. I wanted God to speak to me through it, and many times he did. When I wouldn't know what to do I'd just open the Bible at random and read the first passage my eyes fell upon. I was amazed at how they helped me.

"Then one night I was lying in bed just thinking about a lot of different things, when my body *seemed* to be below me and something within me was rising above it. I looked at my arm, and it looked cold and lifeless, almost dead! And then I came back down. It was quick! But to me it had a significant value. I feel that in God's own way he was trying to tell me that my earthly body isn't important, but rather the spirit inside of me, which one calls a soul! On the night after Halloween my parents had a bonfire for some of their friends in the neighborhood. I stayed outside for a while, but then decided to come in by myself. My parents and I had been having some pretty serious arguments, and I just needed some time to be alone with God and straighten things out. My father had just gotten a new record with "Kum Bah Yah" on it, so I grabbed it on the way up to my bedroom. In my room I turned the lights out and lit some candles. I put the record on and listened very carefully to the words. They seemed to fit.

Someone's crying, Lord . . .
Someone's praying, Lord . . .
Someone's singing, Lord . . .
Come by here my, Lord . . .

I didn't exactly know why but I kept playing the song over and over again.

"After a while I put on the album "Jesus Christ

Superstar" and started praying real hard—more than I ever really had before. I prayed that the Holy Spirit would come into my heart and fill me with complete love.

"I prayed and prayed . . . and then out of the candle came a swirling ball of light, and as I prayed it came towards my body, and seemed to pass into me. Right then I started to shake and convulse. I cried so hard the tears were rolling down my cheeks. I felt *different* inside. Happy. I felt complete, satisfied. I kept praying to the Holy Spirit the whole time.

"My sister came in then and asked me if anything was wrong. I said no and asked her what time it was. From what she told me I had been in my room nearly an hour and a half. I thought I had been there maybe fifteen minutes.

"After it was all over I knew in my heart that the Holy Spirit *was* in me . . . and my faith was strengthened."

"Yes, if you want better insight and discernment, and are searching for them as you would for lost money or hidden treasure, then widsom will be given you, and knowledge of God himself; you will soon learn the importance of reverence for the Lord and of trusting him" (Prov. 2:3-5, Living Bible).

Teen-agers can never be what God intends them to be until Jesus becomes their life and their love.

Teen-agers

I love teen-agers—at least all those that have come my way,
Of those I know, some have wanted to talk, others to pray.

To talk, listen, and pray with one is beautiful and
    refreshing to me.
I love encouraging their faith from the Word of
    God that they might see
How God can work in their lives, if they will permit
    him to
Have his way, and ask him to help them in all they
    do.
Pray, listen, and love them; don't be filled with
    fear.
Commit them to the Lord, trust him, and your
    prayers he will hear.

Chapter VIII

SERVANTS

"Paul, a servant of Jesus Christ."
—Romans 1:1

"Paul and Timotheus, the servants of Jesus Christ,
to all the saints in Christ Jesus"
—Philippians 1:1

"Paul, a servant of God."
—Titus 1:1

Are you God's servant? Paul called himself a
bond servant to Christ. When we permit the Lord
to take over completely in our lives we then become
his servants. He then calls us friends (John 15:15).
As we permit the Lord to direct our lives, we find
our attitudes changing. We *want* to serve others.
We *want* to give of ourselves.

The way in which you serve the Lord each day
may be only to smile. A joyful heart brings forth a
lovely smile. A smile from you may *make* someone's
day. Carolee Shinn said to me the other day, "I
wish people would smile more." She said she had
visited a church several Sundays before and the
sermon was great. She enjoyed everything else
about the church. "But if only the people hadn't

looked so glum." You have to keep in touch with Jesus to have a ready smile. When you read his handbook on life (the Bible) and talk with him, smiles come easily. Several years ago Mrs. Wendell Crum sent me an anonymous statement entitled "The Value of a Smile." One line really impressed me. "It cannot be bought, begged, borrowed or stolen, for it is something that is no earthly good to anybody till it is given away." Please smile! Make people wonder what you have been up to. Serve others with a smile.

I believe the greatest giving of one's self for another that our family has ever experienced was demonstrated through a very dear friend, Bill Lawyer. Our families were very close when we both lived in Waukegan, Illinois. Then our paths separated—they moved to Florida and we to Indiana. We telephoned Bill and his wife Evelyn (who is now with the Lord) and told them about our Becky. This was at the time the doctors said Becky had three months to live. I would like to share excerpts from a letter Bill wrote to us several days after our phone conversation.

"Becky has been on my mind ever since she became ill. After hearing that her doctors had said she had only three months to live I simply could not accept that as the final decision. On my way home from work one Sunday night she came to my thoughts. I did something I had never really done before—I prayed. I would rather say I asked God some questions that had been on my mind for many years. I asked him why it was that a young and beautiful girl like Becky could possibly be taken by him when there are so many who would be willing to go in her place. I told him, *'Take me and leave her here that she might live a full life.* With her personality and her love for music she could direct more people to you than I ever could.' Then I said, 'If you can't do this, then let her live, and I promise you that I will walk in your way for the rest of my life. All you need do is to guide me and you can do anything with me. Thy will be done.' I never thought much more about it until the next morning when you called and said Becky was back in school. Of course, I was so happy for her and for me. I immediately thanked God for answering my first but not last prayer. I also told him I would live up to my promise. I know I'm not worthy of his mercy. I do feel confident he is there. I know he is watching over me and all others.

"You can see the effect your loving daughter has had on my life. I know now that even if she has to be taken my life will be all the better for having known her. I am ashamed that all these years have gone by without my having the peace of mind that passeth all understanding. How simple it is just to ask."

I believe this kind of servant is rare. This type of love for friends is the greatest. Jesus said, "Greater love hath no man than this, that a man lay down his life for his friends" (John 15:13).

I see my friends as Jesus' servants. I am constantly being served. Aren't you? My prayer is that my life be one of giving of myself. I want Christ to be on the throne of my heart; I want to be thinking constantly of others instead of myself. Do you? Read the love chapter often (1 Corinthians 13).

The time has not yet come for Jesus to be with us in person here on earth. He serves us and blesses us through the people with whom he surrounds us. As we serve others we minister to him—the cup of cold water (Matt. 10:42).

Are you aware of the number of servants who serve you daily? The following incidents cite how God constantly supplies servants for my needs.

I came to Hilton Head Island alone to write this book. After I was settled in my room, I felt a twinge of loneliness. At that moment someone tapped on my door saying, "Mrs. Patterson, we have something for you from the desk." A pretty young girl handed me a beautiful bouquet. It was from a dear friend, Sue Hillery. Sue had told me about Hilton Head. The card enclosed in the bouquet said, "Welcome to Hilton Head. God's island and mine." I immediately felt the Lord's presence in this lovely gesture. He was saying, "Betsy, don't be lonely, I'm with you. I instructed one of my servants to do this for you." When God is in a thing you always see perfection, if you are looking. I'm *always* looking!

As I looked around my room it was bright and cheerful with green, yellow, and orange draperies. The bedspreads match the draperies. The lampshades are yellow and white. The carpeting and large comfortable chairs are green. The bouquet is of beautiful yellow mums, tiny white flowers, yellow flowers with orange centers, with beautiful greenery hanging over the edges. The *Lord* chose that bouquet to fit into the decor of the room. He's in everything from the tiniest detail to the greatest. If you are his child, begin to look (if you haven't already) It's all there—little things that make the Christian walk so exciting.

God used Sue in another instance to serve me. It was before I left for South Carolina. I was making a mental list of the things I should take with me. If I just had a little coffee pot, I thought, I could make Sanka in my room. I enjoy a cup before retiring. I knew I didn't have the time to run around town looking for one. For a moment I forgot it. A short time later I was talking to Sue on the phone. She said, "Betsy, I have two things I want to loan you to take on your trip. One is a small coffee pot and cups in a leather case; the other is a very warm but not bulky sweater." I said, "Praise the Lord," and shared my previous thoughts with her. "And it shall come to pass, that before they call, I will answer; and while they are yet speaking, I will hear" (Isa. 65:24).

We earnestly tried to train our children in the knowledge and admonition of the Lord. When our boys married, with God's help, we let go of them. We had obeyed the Lord, and now it was time to commit them into his hands. God has honored our trusting him by supplying servants to further their spiritual education. Several days ago we received a letter from our younger son Mort. I would like to share one paragraph of it with you.

"Becky [his wife] and I are changing our attitudes about a lot of things. It really seems to be helping in many ways. I have started a Bible study time for myself and a program for full tithing. We are finding it is working wonders in our lives, just like you have always said, mom." We praise God for wonderful servants.

I know most of you can identify with some ways God uses his servants when we love our loved ones. When my brother Chester went to be with the Lord a few months ago, his wife Lucile remarked how helpful their hosts of friends had been—God's servants. He sends them to help us over the rough places.

I was ready to leave on a trip to the Holy Land. God used one of his servants to give me a peek into the future. Several days before we were to leave, in my morning quiet time, I read in my devotional book: "Expect a miracle." I said, "Thank you, Lord, I will. When?" No answer came—I had to wait. I had to work at our office that afternoon. When I arrived at the office, Catherine, our secretary, said, "Ruth Eash [another one of God's dear and busy servants] called and asked if she could run in for just a second. She has something for you." Ruth came and told me this story. She had been at her aunt's home the day before. While talking with her aunt she said something about my going to the Holy Land. Ruth said, "My aunt gave me several little mementos for you, and, Betsy, she gave me this. [It was a plaque that said, "Expect a miracle."] Betsy, does this mean anything to you?" I was truly excited when I replied, "I had the same words given to me this morning in my devotional. Ruth, I'm expecting a miracle of some kind on this trip."

It was a jet cruise. We flew to Cypress and then boarded a ship for the remainder of the tour. The ship sailed at night and docked at different ports. One night while we were at sea, Nell Souers and Fran Dickinson, my cabin mates, awakened me. We were in a terrific storm. The boat was rocking up and down. It had thrown Nell out of her bunk. I was on the top bunk above Fran. They helped me down and simultaneously they said, "Let's pray." We talked a moment about how we should pray. We decided on the way Jesus stilled the storm by saying "Peace, be still" (Mark 4:39). Lining up in front of Nell's bunk, we said together, "In Jesus' name, peace be still. Amen." Within five minutes or perhaps even less, the sea was as calm as glass. The *miracle!* Here it was! The miracle I had been promised before I left home. God is the same today as he was yesterday and will be tomorrow (Heb. 13:8). The next morning we learned from the captain that this was the worst storm he had ever experienced. We knew many were praying at the moment we were, but we believe God gave us the key words. I am grateful to Ruth for being an obedient servant. It seemed silly to her at the time to deliver such a plaque to me. God wanted me to recognize his miracle.

I had a similar experience some time later. However, in this instance, I was the obedient servant. I was on a plane flying from Atlanta to Tampa, Florida. Everyone had his tray on his lap, finishing a delicious meal. Suddenly we were in a severe turbulence. The stewardesses were having a difficult time collecting the trays. I could sense that the passengers were getting very nervous and edgy. The captain's voice came over the intercom warning us to fasten our seat belts. I had a window seat. The Lord spoke to me in his still small voice. "You have the power and the words to stop this." "He that believeth on me, the works that I do shall he do also" (John 14:12). I remembered the storm at sea. I looked straight out the window and said quietly aloud, "In Jesus' name, peace be still." Within minutes I saw expressions on faces change from concern to casualness. People relaxed and began talking and laughing once again. I obeyed the voice of the Holy Spirit in faith believing. God does use us as servants in the lives of others if we will permit him that privilege.

This incident of obedience to the Holy Spirit also happened in Jerusalem. Emil and Waddad Abu Dayeh live on the Mount of Olives. Betty Scott, a close friend, and I had Emil as our personal guide when we were in the Holy Land and surrounding areas for seven weeks in 1959. We became much attached to Emil and his family.

This story relates a lesson in obedience and also in answered prayer. Emil owns a tour company. Emil had made various reservations with a company in the States that was booking tours with him. The company in the States went bankrupt, leaving Emil with a debt of about $30,000, which, of course, he really did not owe. He hired a lawyer in the States. The lawyer had the case for a year and hadn't been able to get any money from the bankrupt company for Emil to pay this huge indebtedness. The bus companies, hotels, and others were constantly plaguing him for their money. This was understandable. The responsibility fell upon Emil's shoulders because of his affiliation with this company.

When I arrived on the scene a year and a half ago, Emil and Waddad came to see me at the hotel. We had a lovely visit even though I had a severe cold. When we parted they insisted I come to their home on Sunday morning before we were to leave Jerusalem. Emil said he would come to the hotel and pick me up. I asked him to call me in the morning to see how I was feeling. I felt worse in the morning and really wanted to stay in bed. When he called me, he pleaded with me to come. I finally agreed. Waddad prepared tea for us in her gracious manner. Soon after my arrival Emil began to tell me about the bankruptcy suit and the $30,000 debt. I could see they were both crushed and, naturally, bitter. I silently prayed for wisdom. I told them they might have to accept the situation just as it was before God could change it. I could see from their facial expressions it was going to be very difficult for them to accept. I asked them if I might pray with them about it. They said, "Yes, of course." I don't remember what I prayed, but I know the Holy Spirit put every word upon my lips.

That took place in February. In November of the same year Fran Dickinson returned to Jerusalem. She had promised she would contact Waddad and Emil and greet them for me. When she got into her hotel room, she found that the telephone book was in Arabic. She decided to call the front desk to see if they could tell her how to contact Emil. The operator at the desk said, "Wait just a moment, he's standing here at the desk." A miracle in itself! They made arrangements to meet. After Fran returned home, she excitedly said that Emil had told her to tell me the prayers I prayed with them had been answered.

After I had returned to the States, Emil and Waddad had decided to sell their home so that they might pay the debt. Their children urged them not to do this. Finally they decided against it. Suddenly their business began to flourish so well that from February to November they were able to pay this huge debt. In this particular instance I thanked God I was able to serve him and them.

Being one of God's servants and a friend to others is a rare and beautiful privilege. Have you ever stopped to think how many servants God has sent to you?

Marsh and Sunny Peterson of Waukegan, Illinois, were sent into my life soon after I became a Christian. They were, and still are, never too busy to help or to listen to anyone. Just before Christmas I had to go to the Mayo Clinic because of a physical problem. My husband couldn't leave his practice to go with me. God knew this and immediately supplied a servant, Sunny, to take me and help me in many ways while there. Marsh offered to permit Sunny to go with me, so he, too, was serving God. When we serve God, we serve one another.

I had a week in September, 1973, that without God's servants could have bogged me down and under. It was a fantastic week of walking closely with the Lord. Knowing all that was to transpire during that week, it looked impossible to me. Many of you can identify with me. I reread a wonderful promise in God's word. It said, "My grace is sufficient for thee: for my strength is made perfect in weakness" (2 Cor. 12:9). I believed that promise and I said, "I'm going to trust you Lord to get me through it." God never fails his promises if we trust him.

This is how he honored my trusting. To begin with, I had a physical problem that was causing me much pain. I had a very busy week at my husband's office with secretarial and nursing duties. My oldest brother was critically ill in a nearby city. Then came the joyous news I had been awaiting from Warner Press: "Your book is here," said Dr. Phillips. A local bookstore was making arrangements for an autograph party. I had a speaking engagement out of town. Also a television interview was coming up—all of this in one week along with the usual routine work.

On Friday morning I received the news of my brother's death. God began to get his servants in line and to give each his own particular orders. He first alerted his prayer warriors. They went to prayer in my behalf. He provided our sons and their wives with comforting words that soothed my spirit. I completed all the office work to my satisfaction on Saturday. On Sunday he permitted the pain to increase so that I had to remain in bed, thus having a day when my body could rest.

On Monday he gave me the strength to attend my brother's funeral. From the funeral he sent two servants home with us, my brother Paul and his wife Mary Lou, to look after our family. They performed their duties well—those that had been assigned to them by the Lord. Our house was kept neat, the meals prepared, my hair kept presentable. Mary Lou accompanied me on my speaking engagement and helped sell the books. They also saw to it that I was at the autograph party on time. On the way home from the bookstore after the party, I didn't see how I was going to manage a dinner out with friends which my husband had planned weeks before. At the time we planned it, he didn't know the date of the autograph party. When I arrived home, God had gone before and made the crooked way straight. Earlier in the day my husband had changed the time from 6:00 P.M. to 8:00 P.M. Again *he* was acting as God's servant to me. I had time to lie down, relax, and refresh myself for the evening. This entire week I was looked after and waited upon by God's servants.

God surrounds us with all types of servants. The greatest of all servants is the one who brings the Good News to people. God uses all ages to serve him in this way. This story is how one young man in high school found Christ through another teenager. I call it "the flag story."

Several months ago Carol Seaman called and said she had a wonderful story to tell me. I could tell by the excitement in her voice that this story was a special one. "Betsy, do you remember my telling you about our twenty-five-dollar flag being stolen from our flagpole about a year ago?" "Yes, I do, Carol," I replied. "Just listen to this," she continued. "Yesterday there was a knock on our door. I opened it and there stood a teen-age boy. "Lady," he said, "is your family the one that moved here recently?" "Yes," I said. While speaking to him, I noticed he had something tucked under his arm. He continued, "Did you have a flag stolen from your yard?" "Yes," Carol said, "we did." At that the boy pulled a flag from under his arm and thrust it into her hands. "Lady, I'm the boy who stole it." Carol was flabbergasted. She said, "Why in the world after one whole year would you bring it back?" He hesitated and finally got the words out of his mouth. He exclaimed, "Some boy at Snider High School showed me some things in the Bible that I didn't know were there and I accepted God." Carol, truly elated at this point, invited him into her home. In their conversation she said to him, "I want you to know I'm a Christian, too." The following day she sent a thank-you note and some books to encourage him in his faith.

This story illustrates how a faithful and obedient young servant of the Lord communicated the Good News (the way to inherit eternal life) to one of his own age. That way is through just one person, the Lord Jesus Christ—my life and my love. "I am the way, the truth, and the life: no man cometh unto the Father, but by me" (John 14:6).

Servants

God's people are *servants* wherever they might be,
It was made evident to me quite recently—
A week of activities, how each thing could be accomplished I could not see.

God brought my brother Paul and his wife to me.

They helped in everything, were kept on the run.

The week was over and everything was done.

I still didn't see it until I was out in our boat.

In the stillness of the lily pads came a sob in my
throat.

"God, I understand, all who serve me serve you, oh
Lord."

When they meet you in heaven each will receive his
beautiful reward.

Chapter IX

VISION

"Where there is no vision, the people perish."

—Proverbs 29:18

How do you write a book? This is a question that has been asked of me several times. I asked the same question of Frances Hunter before beginning my first one. She said, "Betsy, hang loose with Jesus." I pondered that phrase many times. I wasn't sure I understood. Some might believe it to be flippant or irreverent. To me that phrase has come alive. I just relax and go aside from everything, reading the Bible and talking with him. Before I begin to write, I have my materials at hand— my Bible, dictionary, and notes of incidents that have happened in my daily walk with him. Then I begin to listen and he directs my mind. I may be mowing the lawn, planting a flower, or standing at my sink. A thought will come. I jot it down on paper and save it. He also leads me as to the exact time I'm to write and even to the place in which I am to write. "In all thy ways acknowledge him, and he shall direct thy paths" (Prov. 3:6).

This chapter was put together so beautifully by him! If I share with you how it was directed by the

Holy Spirit to my listening ear, you will understand
what it means to "hang loose with Jesus."

As I write this chapter I'm spellbound! How he
uses our minds to accomplish any work for him is
thrilling! I must emphasize, however, that our
minds must be completely surrendered to him and
we must be listening. Then his mind works through
ours. I wish to illustrate this by sharing how God
conveyed to me that this chapter was to be written,
and what it was to be about. Then it will be more
meaningful to you.

Having written twelve chapters, I thought the
book was completed. All last week I kept being impressed that two of the chapters were to be omitted. "Lord," I kept repeating, "I won't have enough
material for this book if I omit those two chapters.
But I trust you Lord. You know what you are
doing. I'm just the tool you are using for this
work."

I relaxed knowing he would give me *further in-
structions* when he was ready. I knew I must wait!
"Lead me in thy truth, and teach me ... on thee do
I wait all the day" (Ps. 62:5).

Last Sunday evening I received the "further instructions." My husband and I were watching a
beautiful documentary film on television. It capti-
vated my mind completely. The scenes were some
of God's tremendous handiwork—the beautiful ice
fields in the Antarctic. Watching this I was tuned
in to God. Suddenly a Bible verse came into my
mind and repeated itself again and again: "Where
there is no vision, the people perish" (Prov. 29:18).
"Lord," I asked, "what's this all about?" I glanced
over at my husband. The verse continued to repeat
itself. The Lord then began to impress me with
thoughts which began to jell.

I couldn't have written this chapter in South Carolina because the events and conversations hadn't yet taken place. I've learned to wait until he gives me the go signal.

These are the thoughts he gave me then. They made me realize I was to use this verse, "Where there is no vision, the people perish" and in addition this chapter was to pertain to my husband and the newly opened Burn Unit in St. Joseph's Hospital.

The Lord reminded me that my first book was dedicated to our daughter Becky and that I had written one chapter about Becky. He said, "I had you dedicate this book to Jack, so there is to be one chapter about him and the newly dedicated Burn Unit." I said, "Lord, I'll be happy to obey. Please confirm it again in your Word." The next morning I opened up my devotional book to read the meditation for the day. The scripture verse jumped up at me: "Where there is no vision, the people perish." Thank you, Lord, I said. Later in the day I picked up a book a lady had sent me through the mail and began to read. There was the verse again! "Where there is no vision, the people perish." I said, "That's enough, Lord, I get the message. I *know* you want me to write this chapter."

Three years ago Jack and I attended a seminar on the care of burns at the University of Michigan. We both became very excited about the things we had learned. We felt deep compassion for the burn patients as we were permitted to visit the Burn Unit and observe the treatment and techniques used. Our thoughts were united as to how great it would be if one of Fort Wayne's hospitals could have such a unit.

Jack does most of his surgery and diagnostic procedures at St. Joseph's Hospital (only because providential circumstances have led that way). Arriving back in Fort Wayne the "vision" of a beautiful, effective Burn Unit began to be conceived in my husband's mind. He went to work on it. Needless to say it took months of convincing, planning, and obtaining funds needed for such a venture. It wasn't easy and many times I'm sure he felt it would never come to pass. However, with tremendous help from many people, it finally came into being.

The beautiful Burn Unit was dedicated on February 24, 1974, in St. Joseph's Hospital with a lovely service. It was dedicated to the glory of God! Because of this unit hundreds of people *will not perish* but will continue to live fruitful lives.

Approximately two years ago a man named Frank Koehl was critically burned. My husband treated him. Since his wife Carol is a registered nurse, she helped care for him. It was a long road of pain, skin grafting, discouragement, and depression for Frank. They are a Christian couple and know Jesus, our Great Sustainer. They leaned upon him heavily. Slowly Frank recovered.

I'll never forget the first time he was able to come into the office. I said, "Mr. Koehl, you are a walking miracle." He agreed. I continued, "God must have something very special for you to do for him." He said, "I wonder what it is. I guess I'll just have to wait and see."

Now for the *God incident.* On dedication day of the Burn Unit, I noticed my husband talking with a couple back in the corner. It was the Koehls. We talked about the unit and then I said, "Mr. Koehl, do you remember what I said to you that first day you came into our office after your hospitalization?" He said he did. I replied, "Do you know what it is God wants you to do for him yet?" "No," he said, "but I keep asking." Suddenly I said, "I know what it is. I believe God wants you to come up here to visit the seriously burned patients and talk to them and encourage them. If there are any who do not know our Lord, you might bring a book along to share with them." He excitedly replied, "You know, just before you began telling me, I had the same thoughts go through my mind." I related our conversation to Jack and he was as excited as I was. I said, "You know, honey, Frank stated he would even be willing to show his scars." The total person of ill people should be treated—the soul as well as the body.

Yesterday my husband was on Ann Colone's television program. She gave him the entire program time to speak about the Burn Unit. At the very end Ann announced that something had just occurred which had never before happened in the history of her program while she was interviewing a doctor. She said, "Doctor Patterson has just received an emergency call from the Burn Unit."

I talked with Jack later. He told me this was the first case to be cared for in the unit. It was an eighty-four-year-old man whose clothing had caught on fire from a gas burner. Jack said, "Isn't it strange, Betts, this first patient to come to the unit came while I was speaking about the unit on television." I know God didn't *cause* this to happen. Many things happen to man because he disobeys physical and spiritual laws. I replied, "Perhaps God *permitted* this to happen to alert the people of Fort Wayne to how necessary this Burn Unit is."

I have a wonderful husband! He is an understanding and helpful dad to our children. Since his conversion experience he is like all Christians who are climbing the mountain of the spiritual life. For many years I *had* to be the spiritual head of our home. A young but very mature woman, Jackie Davison, calls this the inverted headship. It is very difficult for me to relinquish this position to him. Each day, with God's help, I'm relinquishing a little more. Each day he is assuming more of his rightful role as the spiritual head. "For the husband is the head of the wife, even as Christ is the head of the church" (Eph. 5:23). We are learning together as the Lord leads us.

My heart is bursting with love for my husband but what I love him for most is that he has relinquished first place in my life to Jesus—my life and my love.

Vision

How great our heav'nly Father is
    when we give him full sway!
In this book, it's stories, truths, and names,
    He has always had his way.
This chapter in particular,
    reflects his loving style.
How he shuffled the written pages around
    has brought me many a smile.
A vision of a Burn Unit
    took form in my husband's mind.
It's finished now, and we're grateful—
    Indiana's only one of its kind.
My husband's prayer and hope now is
    that the total man be fed—
All physical comforts, medical care,
    as well as God's spiritual bread.

Each member of the Unit will
　　assume his sep'rate role,
And a young man, who's been chosen by God,
　　will minister to the soul.

Chapter X

HALLELUJAH

"For the Son of man is as a man taking a far journey, who left his house, and gave authority to his servants, and to every man his work, and commanded the porter to watch. Watch ye therefore: for ye know not when the master of the house cometh, at even, or at midnight, or at the cockcrowing, or in the morning: Lest coming suddenly he find you sleeping. And what I say unto you I say unto all, Watch."

—Mark 13:34-37

Hallelujah! The King is coming! Jesus Christ our Lord and Savior. He did not come into the world to condemn the world but to save man from his sins (John 3:17).

Let me share a chuckle. It came from our older son David's little Davey. David was taking glider lessons. He had received his license. He invited Charlotte (his wife) and Davey to take a ride with him. The tow plane had just let the glider loose and they were gliding along. Davey looked up into his mother's face and said, "Mommy, how are we going to get down?" She gave him an answer that satisfied him. He then said, "Mommy, where's the engine?" She again gave him an answer that satisfied him. Several days later David was preparing to go on a jet flight. (He is in the Air Force.) Davey was back in the bedroom with him while he was packing his bags. Suddenly Davey said, "Daddy, are you going to fly the right way this time?"

After hearing this, I just couldn't help but compare it with Christians. Are we flying the right way or are our lives full of sin? We can answer that only for ourselves. Are your prayers being answered? "If I regard iniquity in my heart, the Lord will not hear me" (Ps. 66:18). Sin (that which is displeasing to God), for example overeating, cuts off our connection with God.

Jesus states he is the bridegroom and Christians are the bride. Think for a moment of the earthly bride and groom. The bride usually prepares for the marriage ceremony months in advance. Her heart's desire is that everything will be as perfect as possible. She shops for her clothing with a watchful eye. She looks for just the right dress, one that will please the groom. Picture in your mind a wedding ceremony. See the bride gliding down the aisle on her father's arm. A picture of perfection! That's the way Jesus wants his bride, which is his church (all believers), to be. The Bible says he wants his bride without spot or blemish (Eph. 5:27). Each of us must take an inward look. Are we sinning? Let's ask God to put his searchlight on our hearts. Ask him to show us our sins, that we might confess them and prepare ourselves for him, the groom. "Search me, O God, and know my heart: try me and know my thoughts: And see if there be any wicked way in me, and lead me in the way everlasting" (Ps. 139:23-24). What peace we will receive in forgiveness! "If we confess our sins, he is faithful and just to forgive us our sins, and to cleanse us from all unrighteousness" (1 John 1:9).

Philippians 2:14 says, "Do all things without murmurings and disputings." Murmuring is complaining; complaining is displeasing to God. Every time you complain about something jot it down on a piece of paper. Here's a sample list: (1) we complain about the weather; (2) we complain about food; (3) we complain about the driver in the car ahead of us; (4) we complain about the number of traffic lights in town. Think of the list you might have at the end of the day. Complaining can become such a habit with us that we do not realize we are doing it. On and on—I'm sure it would be a long list for all of us. Let's ask God to help us stop murmuring and start counting our blessings!

Hebrews 11:6 says that without faith it is impossible to please him. Take a look at your faith. Are you truly trusting in the Lord? Stop and think. If you are concerned about something and find yourself thinking about it much of the time, you are no doubt worrying. Worry is sin. Perhaps you have lost a ring or an important paper. Are you worrying or have you asked the Lord to show you where it is? One day I asked the Lord to give me a promise that I might claim when I lost something. The words came to my mind quickly, "Seek, and ye shall find" (Matt. 7:7). Now whenever I lose something I say, "Lord, you have given me the promise, 'Seek, and ye shall find.'" This morning I claimed that promise. I had lost some important papers. I said, "Lord, you have promised me if I seek I will find." Immediately I was impressed where to look. There they were. We must believe his promises.

Have you ever rescinded a prayer? I did last October. I had prayed that my mother wouldn't die until Jesus came again for the Christians. In mother's last days on earth she became very dizzy and fell several times. My husband had said he didn't see how we could go on like this. I couldn't be with her every minute. He said it looked as if we would have to put her in a nursing home. The morning we took her to the hospital for the last time, I rescinded my prayer for her. I said, "Lord, she has been with us eighteen years. I simply can't put her in a nursing home *now*." I released her into God's hands. He took her to be with him that night. It seemed that I was shedding tears all the time the week before mother's death. I couldn't understand why since there was no apparent reason. After mother died, I realized my grief had gone before. Mother and Grandpa Patterson, who also lived with us, died within seven weeks of each other. His grace is sufficient for our every need (2 Cor. 12:9). If we permit it, "He healeth the broken in heart, and bindeth up their wounds" (Ps. 147:3). He also bottles our every tear and makes a note of them in a book. "Thou tellest my wanderings: put thou my tears into thy bottle: are they not in thy book?" (Ps. 56:8).

If you love and trust the Lord, you give yourself, your time, your talent, and your money to him. A close friend shared with me a new thought. She says that she gives to the Lord's work every new and crispy bill that comes into her hands. In other words, all new money goes to the Lord. Her husband and she have agreed on this. I thought it quite unique. I know the Lord has truly honored and blessed them for this.

When the King comes we want to be ready in every area of our lives. In the area of giving I would like to share this story with you. I suggested a project to our Bible study group. This project was to be our Christmas gift to Jesus. They agreed. We stood in a circle and each of us silently asked the Lord how much money he would have us give. I had a note from a young woman in our group that read as follows. "Enclosed is my money for our gift to Jesus on his birthday. *I* had planned to give maybe ten dollars. The Lord had a different idea. He told me to give my 'carpet money.' I have been saving to buy a new carpet for our little boy's room. I had fifty dollars saved. I didn't like it too well but I said okay, Lord, I'll give it. I quickly thought of what my husband would say. He is a Christian and very generous. I had really been bugging him about that carpet. Now that I had half the money saved I was going to *give it away.* When I told him what the Lord had told me to give he said, 'Terrific, I'll match your amount.' So here's our hundred dollars." A beautiful love gift to Jesus for his birthday, don't you agree? Hallelujah!

One morning Marian Baughman, a new friend of mine, called me and said she wanted to share with me something the Lord had given to her. It was as follows. "When you trust in him, you go with his will. No matter what happens you keep trusting in your heart. You ride the waves of his will and swim the ocean of peace." This shows us how to trust and also the result of trusting (peace). I am truly shocked to hear professing Christians discussing their horoscopes. They check the daily paper to see what is supposed to take place in their lives on that particular day. Are we trusting God when we are trusting in other things? "Thou shalt have no other gods before me" (Exod. 20:3).

If we want to be ready when the King comes, we should have a knowledge of the Bible—his book.

Immerse yourself in the Word of God. When you do that you are immersing yourself in Jesus. Jesus is the Word (John 1:1-2). Fill every free chink of time with prayer or with reading God's Word. You can carry a small Testament in your purse or pocket. Whenever you have to wait for someone or something, get your Testament out and read. Try praying while waiting at a stop light (don't close your eyes). This is good spiritual exercise.

Here is a paragraph that a friend gave me one time. It has been one of my most valuable assets. The author is unknown. Perhaps it will be a help to you.

"Satan rushes men. God leads them. Never act in panic, nor allow men to dictate to you. Calm yourself and be still. Force yourself into the quiet of your closet until your pulse beats normally and the scare has ceased to distress you. When you are most eager to act is the time you will make the most pitiful mistakes. Do not say in your heart what you will or will not do. Wait upon God until he makes known his way. So long as that way is hidden, it is clear that there is no need to act and that God accounts himself responsible for all the results of keeping you where you are."

Hallelujah, the King is coming! "Which in his times he shall show, who is the blessed and only Potentate, the King of kings, and Lord of lords" (1 Tim. 6:15). I have a precious four-year-old friend, Holly Seaman. Holly is preparing for the King's coming. She is memorizing Bible verses. She has memorized the Twenty-Third Psalm and John 3:16. Several weeks ago I was ill. Holly and her mother came to see me. She has called me Patterson since our first meeting. She came back to the bedroom to say hi and then went out to our family room with Angie. Just before they left, Holly told me she wanted to pray for me. She said, "Dear Jesus, heal Patterson. Amen." Short, but she had said all that was needed. Carol and Max are training Holly for the King's coming. "Train up a child in the way he should go: and when he is old, he will not depart from it" (Prov. 22:6). Perhaps just now as you are reading this you are concerned over one of your family, who is away from the daily fellowship with the Lord. This promise never fails. "Commit thy way unto the Lord; trust also in him; and he shall bring it to pass" (Ps. 37:5).

Thousands of young people are studying God's Word and witnessing for him. I was told a story some months ago that truly proves God is certainly working with the youth of today.

Some students at a nearby college invited a person who professes to be an atheist to come to their college. They asked her if she would participate in a debate on the subject "Christianity versus atheism." She accepted. The various students gave their comments on Christianity. The atheist expressed her views and summarized her thoughts on atheism. The leader of the college debate team gave the summary for their side of the question. This is what he said. "Dear lady, if we are wrong in what we believe, we have *nothing* to lose, but if you are wrong in your beliefs, you have *everything* to lose." This story had a tremendous effect upon me. Perhaps it will speak to you if you are not a Christian.

Do you know Jesus the King of kings personally? If you would die this minute would you go to heaven? I'm not trying to frighten you, but we must face reality. *You can know!* Confess all your past sins, and then ask Jesus to come into every area of your life. Believe by faith he has done as you have asked. It is as simple as that. "He that believeth on the Son hath everlasting life: and he that believeth not the Son shall not see life; but the wrath of God abideth on him" (John 3:36). To go to heaven and spend all eternity in perfect bliss with God is a free gift to anyone who will accept the gift. "For by grace are ye saved through faith; and that not of yourselves: it is the gift of God: not of works, lest any man should boast" (Eph. 2:8-9).

The King is coming! The question is not When? but Are you ready? Prepare yourself for his coming. Make him your love and your life.

Hallelujah

Hallelujah the King is coming!
Are you laughing, praying, and rejoicing?
It's not *When?* but *Are you ready?*
You should be if you're true to him and steady.
The one requirement is to be born again
And then give your life to spend
On others until he comes.
People will come alive and some
Will go on and touch others too.
It's like a pebble thrown into the ocean blue—
On and on the *good news* spreads
Until it becomes people's daily bread.
God loves you are the words—
Sheer magic—if they are heard.
Around the world the command he gives,
So we must heed this call of his
Hallelujah, the King is coming, Jesus is his name.
All bow down and worship him, all in Christ are the same.

2 Corinth. 12-9 My Grace is
sufficient for thee